CHARLIE BROWN'S
'CYCLOPEDIA

Super Questions and Answers and Amazing Facts

Featuring
Boats and Other Things
that Float

Volume 5

Based on the Charles M. Schulz Characters

Funk & Wagnalls, Inc.

Photograph and Illustration Credits: Capt. Bartlett/American Museum of Natural History, 197; John M. Christensen, 225 (top left); Copyright 1978 The Cousteau Society, 231, 237; Cunard Lines, 214, 215; Danish Tourist Board, 234; Eleanor Ehrhardt, 219, 228, 229; Giorgio Gualco/Bruce Coleman, Inc., 195; Hawaii Visitors' Bureau, x; Ed McGill, 223, 225 (bottom); The Metropolitan Museum of Art Excavations, 1919-20, Rogers Fund, Supplemented by Contribution of Edward S. Harkness, 199; Missouri Historical Society, 211; Moran Inland Waterways Corporation, 219; National Oceanic and Atmospheric Administration, National Ocean Survey, 232; New York City Fire Department Photo Unit, 220, 222; The New-York Historical Society, 212; Norwegian Information Service, 194; Nova Scotia Communications and Information Centre, 207, 235; Walter T. Otto, Jr., 227; Plimoth Plantation, Plymouth, Massachusetts, 206; I. N. Phelps Stokes Collection, Prints Division, The New York Public Library, Astor, Lenox and Tilden Foundation, 210; Swedish Information Service, 201; U. S. Navy, 236, 238, 239, 240; United States Virgin Islands, 225 (top right).

A large part of the material in this volume was previously published in *Charlie Brown's Third Super Book of Questions and Answers.*

Introduction

Welcome to volume 5 of *Charlie Brown's 'Cyclopedia*! Have you ever wondered what a galleon is, or what the first boats were like, or what a harbor pilot does? Charlie Brown and the rest of the *Peanuts* gang are here to help you find the answers to these questions and many more about all kinds of boats and other things that float. Have fun!

Charlie Brown on the Sea

How did people first cross rivers and streams?

If the water was too deep to walk through, they probably swam. But only the strongest swimmers could have gotten across a wide river. Some early, tired swimmer probably grabbed onto a floating log. He or she became the first person to use a raft— a simple platform that floats on water.

What were early rafts like?

One log, and then two logs tied together, were probably the first rafts. A rider had nothing to paddle with but his hands. Later a person most likely used a stick to push the raft through the water. Still later people discovered that a flat piece of wood worked better than a stick. It made the raft go faster. And so the paddle was invented.

In some parts of the world people built other kinds of rafts. In Egypt, for example, they tied together bundles of sticks or heavy reeds.

"Kon-Tiki"

What is the "Kon-Tiki"?

The "Kon-Tiki" is one of the most famous rafts in the world. It was built in 1947 by Thor Heyerdahl (HI-ur-doll), a Norwegian scientist. The "Kon-Tiki" is a copy of the rafts used by natives of the South Pacific. It is made of balsa, a light wood that floats easily. Heyerdahl sailed the tiny "Kon-Tiki" thousands of miles across the Pacific Ocean. He went from South America to Polynesia (pol-uh-NEE-zhuh)—a group of islands south of Hawaii. Heyerdahl's voyage proves that people could have made the same trip by raft 1,500 years ago. So it is possible that the people of Polynesia are the great, great, great . . . grandchildren of South American Indians.

What were the first boats like?

The first boats developed from rafts. To keep dry, people turned up the sides of their reed rafts. In this way, they invented a saucer-shaped boat. Then people made longer, narrower boats. Long boats are easier to steer than round ones. The narrower shape allows boats to move through the water faster.

What is a canoe?

A canoe is a long, narrow boat that is pointed at both ends. One, two, or three people sit in the canoe, facing the front, or bow (rhymes with cow). They use a paddle, or paddles, to move the canoe through the water and steer it. Canoes were among the first kinds of small boats.

What did the earliest Americans use when they traveled by water?

The earliest Americans, Indians, used canoes. They had two kinds—dugout and birchbark. Which kind of canoe they used depended on where they lived. In the north, where birch trees grew, Indians made birchbark canoes. In other places they made dugouts.

How did the Indians make a dugout canoe?

A dugout canoe was made from a long, thick log. The canoe-maker burned the middle of the log partway through. Then he scraped or dug out the inside to make it hollow.

Dugout canoes are very heavy, and move slowly through the water. But they are very strong.

What is a birchbark canoe like?

A birchbark canoe is made of bark strips peeled from birch trees. The person making the canoe sews the strips together, using tree roots for thread. He then attaches the bark to a wooden frame.

Birchbark canoes are much lighter than dugout canoes. They can be carried easily from one stream to another. Dugout canoes are too heavy to be carried very far.

 In 1928, a man crossed the Atlantic Ocean in a canoe with a sail. The trip took 58 days!

Are canoes still used today?

Yes, people still use canoes. In certain places, such as Africa and the South Pacific islands, people still travel by canoe. But in most other parts of the world, canoes are used mainly for fun. People take them on hunting or fishing trips or on camping holidays. Today, most canoes are made by machine, not by hand. And they are not all made of wood. Now some canoes are made of canvas, light metal, or plastic.

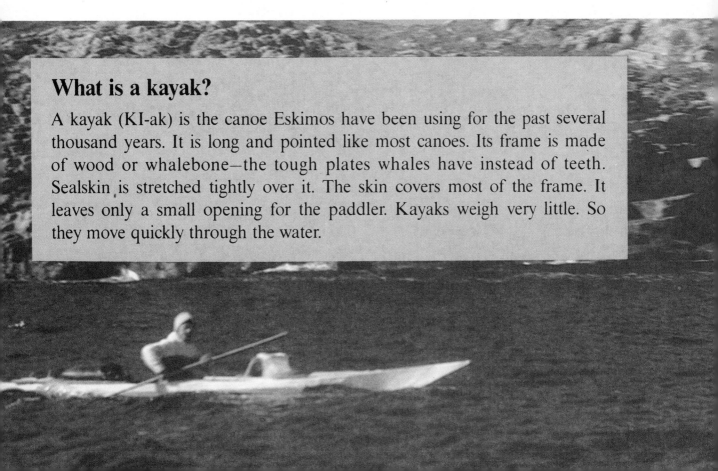

What is a kayak?

A kayak (KI-ak) is the canoe Eskimos have been using for the past several thousand years. It is long and pointed like most canoes. Its frame is made of wood or whalebone—the tough plates whales have instead of teeth. Sealskin is stretched tightly over it. The skin covers most of the frame. It leaves only a small opening for the paddler. Kayaks weigh very little. So they move quickly through the water.

What is a rowboat?

A rowboat is any kind of boat that is moved by oars. An oar is longer than a paddle, but it's used in the same way. A simple rowboat seats one person. The rower usually uses two oars, one on each side of the boat. Many rowboats have oarlocks to hold the oars in place.

WHY DO YOU HAVE TO MAKE A BIG DEAL OUT OF EVERYTHING... I JUST SAID I'D TAKE YOU ROWING.

Why did people add sails to their boats?

A sail on a boat can catch the wind. This, in turn, causes the boat to move. The ancient Egyptians discovered this fact about 5,000 years ago. The first sails were made of thick materials that could trap the wind. Either a large square piece of linen or papyrus (puh-PIE-russ)—a heavy, coarse paper— was used.

The early sailors could travel only *with* the wind. If the wind was blowing in the wrong direction, they had to put down their sails and row the boat themselves. It was not until the triangular sail was invented that sailing in almost any direction became possible. This happened about 1,600 years ago.

Who were the first sailors to use ships?

The first people to use ships lived around the Mediterranean (med-ih-tuh-RAY-nee-un) Sea. Many of these people were from Egypt and Phoenicia (fih-NISH-uh), a land where Syria, Lebanon, and Israel are today.

The Egyptians started to do a great deal of sailing more than 4,000 years ago. They made easy-to-sail ships from wooden boards. They sailed these ships around the Mediterranean, trading with other countries. Then, about 3,000 years ago, the Phoenicians began to design ships both for trading and for fighting sea battles. They made long, fast ships for fighting. They made short, wide ones for trading.

Model of Egyptian galley ship rowed by slaves

Were ships ever built that used 50 oars?

One of the earliest ships, known as a galley, sometimes had 50 or more oars. Galleys were first used by the people who lived around the Mediterranean Sea more than 3,000 years ago. Galleys were rowed by slaves who sat on benches. Each man held an oar with both hands. And all the slaves rowed at the same time. The earliest galleys had no sails. But later ones did. Even so, their most important source of power was muscle. Most galleys also had one large oar at the back of the boat. It was used for steering.

Early Romans believed that ships needed eyes to see. So they painted eyes on their galleys!

What's the difference between boats and ships?

Boats are smaller than ships. And they rarely travel far out on the ocean. Ships do. They are large, seagoing vessels. Ships are used for trading, carrying passengers, and fighting battles.

Who thought of using more than one sail?

About 2,500 years ago, both the Greeks and the Phoenicians came up with a new idea in ship design. Until then, ships had always had one mast (pole for a sail) and one sail. The Greeks and the Phoenicians added a second mast and two more sails. The added sails gave them extra speed and better control of direction. About 2,000 years later, the Greeks added a third mast and a fourth sail.

Who were the Vikings?

The Vikings were fierce seagoing pirates from Norway, Denmark, and Sweden. They traveled by sea to raid other parts of Europe about 1,000 years ago. They probably traveled as far as America before the time of Columbus! The Vikings made some permanent settlements in England, Russia, Iceland, and Greenland.

The Vikings founded the city of Dublin, Ireland!

What kind of ships did the Vikings use?

Viking warships were long, narrow, and fast. They were usually open on top and had flat oak bottoms. They had many oars and just one sail. The earliest of these were called long ships. However, the later Viking ships were longer than the long ships. Each of these later ships had a wood carving at the front. The carving was of a person's head or of a monster, such as a dragon. The Vikings called these warships "drakkars"—dragons.

The Vikings had other kinds of ships, too. A wider ship, called a knorr (pronounce the "k"), carried goods for trading. Knorrs had fewer oars, so there was more room for cargo.

Why did people put "figureheads" on their ships?

Some figureheads served the same purpose as a name painted on a ship. They were used to identify the ship. Figureheads were also used to scare away evil spirits. Dragon heads and other monsters were common on Viking ships for that reason.

HEY, SISTER, I THINK YOU MISSED YOUR CALLING...YOU WOULD HAVE MADE A GREAT FIGUREHEAD!

Why is the right side of a ship called "starboard" and the left called "port"?

The Vikings were the first to use those names. A typical Viking ship had a giant steering oar. It was on the right side, near the back of the ship. It was there for two reasons. First, most people are right-handed. Second, the ancient people believed that the right side of a ship was stronger than the left side. The right side of a Viking ship was eventually called the "steerboard." We've changed it a little, to "starboard."

Because the steering oar was in the way, the Vikings could not dock on the right side of the ship. They always docked with the left side facing port. So that's what they called it—and so do we.

Why did Columbus sail west to get to the East?

Christopher Columbus believed that the world was round. Before his time (the late 1400s), just about everyone had assumed the world was flat. If the world really was round, Columbus thought, he should be able to reach the Indies—east of Europe—by sailing west. (The "Indies" was a name for India, China, and the islands of Southeast Asia.) In fact, Columbus believed the shortest route would be directly west across the Atlantic Ocean.

When Columbus reached America for the first time, he thought he was in the Indies. That's why he named the people there Indians!

202

What kind of ships did Christopher Columbus use for his famous 1492 voyage?

Two of Columbus's ships, the "Niña" and the "Pinta," were caravels. These light, fast sailing ships first became popular around 1400. They had three masts: the foremast (in the front), the mainmast (in the middle), and the mizzenmast (in the back). The foremast had a square sail. But the other two masts had sails in the shape of triangles.

The third ship—and the largest—was a carrack. Known as the "Santa María," it was the one Columbus himself traveled on. The ship had the same three masts as the caravels. But both the mainmast and the foremast had square sails. Only the mizzenmast had a sail in the shape of a triangle. A pole called a bowsprit stuck out from the front, or bow, of the ship. It held a small square sail.

Where did Columbus's crew sleep?

On the floor! Only the most important officers of the "Niña," the "Pinta," and the "Santa María" slept in bunks. The other men had to sleep on deck. However, after Columbus's first voyage to America, the men slept below deck in hammocks. The hammock was an American Indian invention which Columbus and his men adopted.

Mainmast

Foremast

Mizzenmast

Bowsprit

The "Santa María"

What is a galleon?

A galleon is a large wooden sailing ship which was popular in Europe during the mid-1500s. It was used for trading and, in wartime, for battle. A galleon was better for long-distance sea voyages than earlier sailing ships. It was much deeper. So it had bunk space for the whole crew.

The foremast and the mainmast of a galleon each have two or three sails. Sometimes the mizzenmast has two sails, also. Some of the early galleons had oars as well as sails. But galleons could be rowed only in smooth waters.

Was Magellan the first person to sail around the world?

Ferdinand Magellan always gets the credit. However, he never actually completed the trip around the world. But one of his ships did.

Magellan was a Spanish-Portuguese sailor. In 1519, he decided to try to find a short route to the Indies. He planned to go around the tip of South America and then west to Asia.

He left Spain with five ships. In two years Magellan got halfway around the world. During the voyage he was killed on a Pacific island. Of his five ships only one completed the trip. One ship was wrecked on a rock. One returned to Spain early when its crew mutinied (rebelled against Magellan). One was left, leaking badly, on a Pacific island. And one was lost on the way home.

What was the Spanish Armada?

For many years, no country was as mighty as Spain when it came to ocean travel. During the 1500s, Spain had the largest fleet of ships in Europe. It was known as the Spanish Armada. These ships were used by Spanish explorers to sail across the Atlantic Ocean to America. The Spaniards brought back many treasures from the New World. Spain became a very rich country.

The Armada also protected Spain from enemies and fought her battles when it was necessary. Because of its Armada, Spain was, for many years, one of the most powerful countries in Europe. But in 1588, a fleet of English ships defeated the Spanish Armada. The English then were masters of the sea.

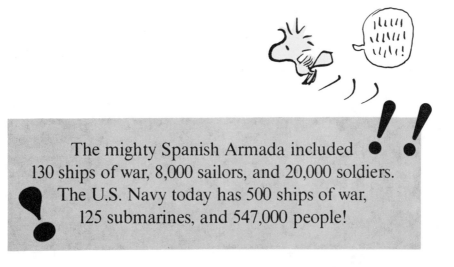

The mighty Spanish Armada included 130 ships of war, 8,000 sailors, and 20,000 soldiers. The U.S. Navy today has 500 ships of war, 125 submarines, and 547,000 people!

What kind of ship was the "Mayflower"?

The ship that carried the Pilgrims to the New World in 1620 was a fairly small trading ship. She was about 90 feet (27 meters) long. That's about the length of six taxicabs lined up in a row. Some passengers on the "Mayflower" slept in bunks along the sides of the ship. Others made their beds on the floor of the covered deck. The upper part of the ship had many leaks. So the Pilgrims often felt ice-cold water splashing on them.

Before she carried passengers, the "Mayflower" had carried wine. So the ship's hold (the place where the cargo is kept) smelled quite sweet. Most ships of that time smelled of garbage and damp cargo.

The voyage of the "Mayflower" from England to Massachusetts took more than two months. Today you can fly the same distance on an SST airplane in three and a half hours!

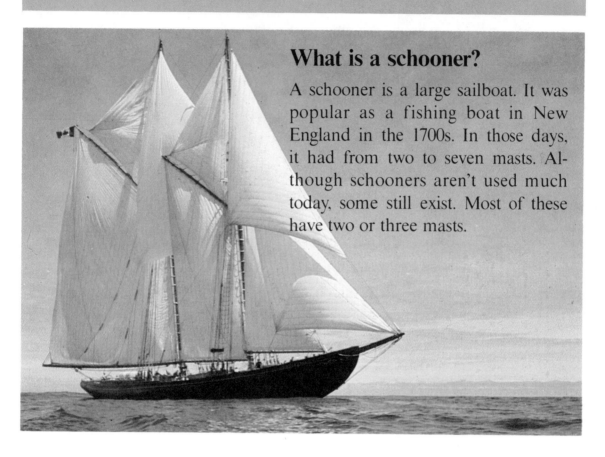

What is a schooner?

A schooner is a large sailboat. It was popular as a fishing boat in New England in the 1700s. In those days, it had from two to seven masts. Although schooners aren't used much today, some still exist. Most of these have two or three masts.

What does the word "schooner" mean?

The name "schooner" comes from a game that was popular when the schooner was first designed in 1713. Young boys used to throw flat stones in the bay and watch them skip along the water. They called this game "scooning." ("Scoon" is a Scottish word for "glide.") People say that when one of the new sailing boats first appeared, someone shouted, "See how she scoons!" The name stuck—even though the word is spelled differently today.

I FIND IT HARD TO BELIEVE THAT SKIPPING THOSE ROCKS CAN AMUSE YOU FOR HOURS ON END...

TYPICAL REACTION OF A NON "SCHOONER!"

What were the first ships to run on a regular schedule?

The first regularly scheduled ships were packet ships. These passenger ships became popular in the mid-1800s. Before this time, ships sailed only when conditions were right. They had to have full loads of both cargo and passengers. And the weather had to be good. Packet ships sailed at a set time no matter what! Their owners also made an effort to see to it that first-class passengers were comfortable. So, packet ships were popular with rich ocean travelers. No other shipowners had bothered much about passengers before.

What were the fastest sailing ships?

Clipper ships were the fastest and the most beautiful of the great sailing ships. Both their beauty and their speed came from the way they were built. They had long, sleek bodies and a large number of sails. Some clippers had as many as 35 sails.

Clipper ships were used during the mid-1800s. At that time the United States and East Asia (especially China) were doing a great deal of trading. Clippers carried tea, coffee, and spices. These things would spoil if they remained on board ship for too long a period of time. So speed was very important. Clipper ships were named for the way they could "clip off the miles." A clipper could make a trip from the east coast of the United States to China and back in six months. It had to travel all the way around the tip of South America to get to the Pacific Ocean. So six months was a record time in those days.

Were windjammers a kind of ship?

Yes, windjammers were iron sailing ships with four masts. They became popular just after clipper ships. They, too, were used for trading and carrying cargo from East Asia. Windjammers were huge and strong. They were perfect for sailing in bad weather and rough seas.

When did people start using steamboats?

The first workable steamboat was built in 1787 by an American named John Fitch. The boat had six long paddles on each side—like a big canoe! The paddles were moved by a steam engine.

Three years later, Fitch improved his model and put the paddles at the back. He then started taking passengers and cargo up and down the Delaware River. However, the engine was so large, there was very little room for the cargo. And not many people were interested in traveling on a steamboat. So Fitch's steamboat service failed.

What was "Fulton's Folly"?

In 1807 Robert Fulton built the "Clermont," the first successful steamboat. People thought that building a steamboat was a foolish idea. So they called the boat "Fulton's Folly." But building the "Clermont" turned out to be a smart idea—not a foolish one. Fulton had combined the best features from steamboats other people had invented. Before long, the "Clermont" was making regular trips along the Hudson River in New York.

"Clermont" on the Hudson River

What did the "Clermont" look like?

This is a picture of the "Clermont." Even though it had a bulky steam engine, the boat carried two masts with sails—just in case. It also had a smokestack that coughed out black smoke. It did not have canoe paddles like those on John Fitch's steamboat. Instead, the "Clermont" had a paddle wheel on each side.

210

Though the "Clermont" had room to seat 24 passengers, only 14 people were brave enough to go on its first trip. Yet one month later, 90 passengers crowded on board!

What is a paddle wheel?

A paddle wheel is a huge wheel with a series of flat paddles attached to it. On a moving steamboat, part of the wheel was always underwater. The power from a steam engine turned the wheel forward. As the paddles pushed against the water, they moved the boat forward.

What was a showboat?

A showboat was a paddle-wheel steamboat used as a traveling theater. In the 1800s, gaily decorated showboats brought plays, circuses, and live music to towns along the Mississippi River. Some boats even carried zoos and museums! Often the show was held right on the boat. But sometimes the showboat pulled a flat boat, called a barge, behind it. Then the theater was on the barge.

Why don't we see paddle-wheel boats any more?

Because the paddle wheel was replaced by the propeller. Starting in 1816, some steamboats used propellers. Others still had paddle wheels. Great arguments took place as to which was better. In 1845 two nearly identical British ships had a series of contests. The "Rattler" had a propeller. The "Alecto" had a paddle wheel. The "Rattler" won every race. Soon after that. propellers replaced paddle wheels. Propellers are still used on ships today.

Where were paddleboats used?

Mostly on rivers. There is less wind over a river than over an ocean. Therefore, sailboats move slowly on rivers. But steamboats can move quickly. In America steamboats became very popular on the great Mississippi and Ohio rivers.

"Savannah"

What was the first steamship to cross the Atlantic?

The paddle-wheeler "Savannah." In 1819 she left her home port in Georgia for Liverpool, England. Many people believed that such a "steam coffin" would never make it all the way across the Atlantic Ocean. But she did—29 days later.

Twenty-nine days was not a record time for a ship to cross the Atlantic. Any packet ship of the day could have made the trip in that amount of time—or even less. Why wasn't the trip faster? The "Savannah" was built as a sailing ship. Her steam engine and paddle wheels were added later. Most of the first Atlantic crossing was made using sail power. The "Savannah" had only enough fuel to run her engine for about 85 hours (less than four days). Her trip was a first—but only a small beginning for steam.

The first all-steam ship crossing took place 19 years later. The "Sirius" (SIR-ee-us) made the trip from Ireland to the east coast of the United States in 18½ days. By the 1840s many steamships were making trips across the Atlantic Ocean.

213

Do we still use steamships today?

Yes. You have probably seen pictures of huge ocean liners, like the "Queen Elizabeth 2." You may even have seen some of the actual liners. You can recognize them by their large smokestacks. Most ships with a smokestack are steamships. But some modern ships have diesel engines, and others are run by atomic energy.

How long does it take a steamship to cross the ocean today?

A fast steamship can cross the Atlantic Ocean between New York and Southampton, England, in 5½ days.

It takes about 12 days for a fast steamship to cross the Pacific Ocean from Seattle, Washington, to Kobe, Japan.

Is a trip on a modern ocean liner any fun?

Yes! A modern ocean liner is like a floating hotel. Once on board, it's easy to forget you're on a ship. The rooms are something like hotel rooms. And every modern convenience is right at your fingertips. There are restaurants, shops, game rooms, elevators, theaters, gymnasiums, and swimming pools. Some liners even have tennis courts!

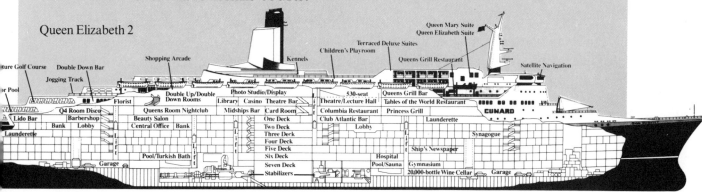

Queen Elizabeth 2

What's the difference between a port and a harbor?

Sometimes people use the words "port" and "harbor" to mean the same thing. But there is a difference. All ports are harbors, but not all harbors are ports.

A harbor is part of a body of water that is deep enough for anchoring boats or ships. It is partly surrounded by land. Or else it has man-made piers that stick out into the water. The land or the piers protect boats from strong winds and rough water currents.

A port is a special kind of harbor. Passengers and freight can be loaded or unloaded there. A large, busy port usually has cranes for handling heavy freight, warehouses for storing things, radio equipment, repair services, fueling stations, and even restaurants.

What is a cargo ship?

A cargo ship carries goods for trading. The old clipper ships were cargo ships. They carried tea and spices from China to America. They needed to be fast so that the cargo would not spoil before it could be unloaded. Today many cargo ships have refrigerators on them. So there is no spoilage problem.

Modern cargo ships are divided into four categories, according to the things they carry. General cargo ships carry things that are put in packages, such as food, machinery, and clothing. Tankers carry oil or other liquids. Dry bulk carriers carry unpackaged goods like coal or grain. Multipurpose ships carry a few different kinds of cargo at once.

216

How are cargo ships loaded and unloaded?

Large electric cranes lift boxes and barrels onto and off of general cargo ships. Once the cargo is aboard, crew members store it in various places in the ship.

Some general cargo ships called container ships carry all the cargo in large, weatherproof metal boxes. Container ships are the quickest to load and unload. Cranes drop the boxes directly into special compartments on the ship where the boxes fit neatly. So, few crew members are needed to do the job. Later, each box is put on the trailer part of a tractor-trailer truck. Or else it is loaded right onto a railroad flatcar.

Oil is pumped on and off a tanker through special hoses.

What's a supertanker?

A supertanker is a very large oil-carrying tanker. It is the largest kind of non-military ship that exists. Picture three football fields in a row. Many supertankers are longer even than that! Supertankers are slower than other types of large ships. But they provide the cheapest way to carry oil.

217

What is a tramp ship?

Like a person we call a tramp, a tramp ship travels around looking for any work it can find. Most cargo ships carry their loads on a regular schedule and over a special route. A tramp ship is a cargo ship with no fixed schedule or route. It travels from port to port, taking whatever work is available. It goes wherever cargo needs to be taken.

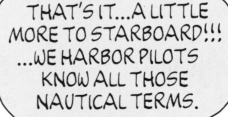

What is a harbor pilot?

When a ship comes into or leaves a port, a harbor pilot must be on board. His job is to guide the ship through the harbor waters. The pilot must be familiar with the tides, the winds, and all the markers in the harbor's waters. The markers tell the pilot where the water is shallow or where there are dangerous rocks.

What do tugboats do?

Tugboats are small, powerful boats. They are used to tow and guide bigger boats and ships into or out of a harbor. Most tugs are used to pull large ocean liners and cargo ships through shallow waters or narrow areas. Without the tugs, large ships have a hard time moving through such places. Some tugs tow damaged ships into the harbor.

Modern tugboats get their power from diesel engines, like the ones used in locomotives. But in the 1800s, tugs were driven by steam-powered paddle wheels.

What does a fireboat do?

A fireboat puts out fires on ships and piers. Most big ports have at least one fireboat. It is equipped with powerful "water guns" that shoot great streams of water at the fire. A nozzle at the top of a tall tower shoots water the farthest. It can aim water at the deck or the inside of a burning ship. When big passenger liners come into the harbor, fireboats sometimes greet them by spraying water high into the air.

What is a dry dock?

In order for a ship to be repaired and painted, it must be taken out of the water. Since large ships are heavy, special docks called dry docks were invented for the purpose. There are two main kinds—the floating dock and the graving dock.

The floating dry dock is a floating platform with walls on two sides. Water is pumped into it. The dock sinks, and the ship moves onto it. When the water is pumped out again, the dock rises once more to the surface. Now the ship is in dry dock.

The graving dry dock is a deep concrete tub sunk into the ground. One end of it opens into the harbor. When the ship enters, a gate closes it off from the harbor. Then water is pumped out. The ship sinks with the water. When all the water has been pumped out, the ship is in dry dock.

What is a barge?

A barge is a flat-bottomed boat used to carry heavy freight, like coal or steel. It usually has square ends that make docking and unloading easy.

In the old days, barges had no motors. They were pulled by horses or oxen. The animals would walk on the land next to the river or canal, pulling ropes attached to the barge. (Now this towing work is usually done by other boats.) Some modern barges have their own motors. These barges can carry up to 20 million pounds (9 million kilograms), of freight.

What kind of boat is a ferry?

A ferry is a boat that carries passengers across a small body of water, like a lake or a river. Some ferries carry people across even larger bodies of water. However, all ferries travel back and forth between two ports on a regular schedule. Some ferry rides take five minutes. Others take two days. The ferries that make long trips have dining rooms and sleeping compartments.

Ferries often carry more than passengers. Some are large enough to carry cars or even railroad trains.

Most ferries are run by diesel or steam engines. But in some places, you can find ferries that are pushed along with poles. Others are pulled by men or animals on a nearby shore or river bank.

Ferries that carry trains across a body of water have their own tracks. So a whole train can ride right onto a train ferry and then ride off again!

What are gondolas?

Gondolas are long, thin rowboats often used as water taxis. They are popular in Venice, Italy. Instead of roads, most of Venice has canals—narrow inland waterways. So people there use boats instead of cars to travel from place to place.

At the back of a gondola stands the gondolier—the man who runs the boat. He uses a long, narrow pole to push his gondola through the shallow canals.

Is a junk a rotten old boat?

Junk

No. A junk is a kind of wooden sailboat. It was first used by the Chinese a few hundred years ago. If you go to the Orient today, you will still see many junks. They are usually painted in bright colors. White circles on the front stand for eyes. They are the boats' guiding spirits that watch for dangers.

Junks have flat bottoms and high sterns (backs). They have two or more four-cornered sails. Compared to modern boats, junks are slow and hard to handle. That's why some people have put outboard motors on their junks.

223

What is a catamaran?

A catamaran is a sailboat made by joining two separate hulls together. A little space is left between them. "Cats," as these strange-looking boats are called, are very fast. The two hulls give them excellent balance.

Catamarans were invented by people who lived in the South Seas—a part of the Pacific Ocean. There the natives used logs to make the two hulls. They used paddles and sometimes added sails to make their cats move. The South Sea natives used catamarans to carry things over long distances. Some people still use catamarans today.

What is a sampan?

A sampan is a small, fast-moving boat found in China, Japan, and other nearby countries. A sampan is often used as a house for a family. Some sampans are also used for carrying things to be sold.

Not all sampans look alike. But most have a cabin that is covered with straw mats. The cabin is where people usually sleep. Most sampans have oars and sails. If there's no wind for sailing, the owners can always row.

Where is there a floating sampan "city"?

In Hong Kong, a British colony on the south coast of China. Here groups of people live or work on sampans, docked one right next to the other. Some sampans are homes. Others are food stores or restaurants. Many of the sampans are very old. Their cabin covers are full of patches.

Sampan

Catamaran

Sampan City

Do any people in the U.S. live on boats?

Some Americans live on floating homes called houseboats. Houseboats don't usually have power of their own. To travel from one place to another, they have to be towed by a second boat. Some families in the warmer parts of the United States live on houseboats all year round. Other people rent houseboats just for the summer months or for an even shorter period of time. Still others spend their summers on yachts.

The largest private sailing yacht ever built was the "Sea Cloud." It was owned by Mrs. Marjorie Merriweather Post, a very wealthy woman. The "Sea Cloud" was 350 feet (105 meters) long —longer even than the largest sailing ships ever built!

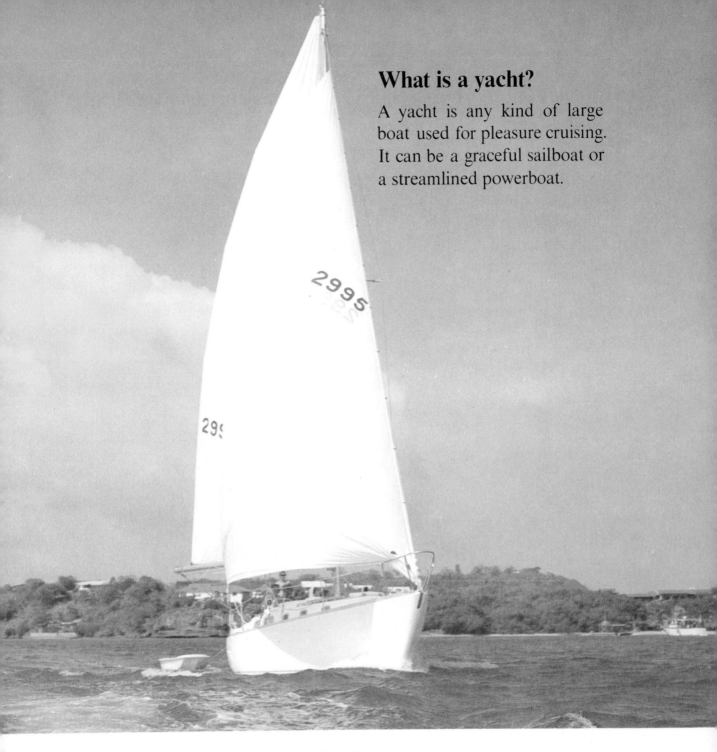

What is a yacht?

A yacht is any kind of large boat used for pleasure cruising. It can be a graceful sailboat or a streamlined powerboat.

What do sailing yachts look like?

Here are the pictures of three sailing yachts—a yawl, a ketch, and a schooner. These all have two masts and three or more sails. Most yachts are longer than 5 taxicabs in a row. Some are even longer than 20 taxicabs in a row!

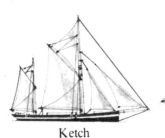

Ketch

Schooner

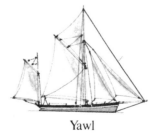

Yawl

227

How did sailing ships help to celebrate America's 200th birthday?

Two hundred twenty-six sailing ships from all over the world came to New York City on July 4, 1976, and paraded up the Hudson River. The parade was called Operation Sail 1976, or Op Sail '76. It was part of America's 200th birthday celebration.

Only 20 tall sailing ships with square sails were left in the world at that time. Sixteen of them took part in Op Sail. So did 60 naval ships from 40 countries, and 150 other large ships. Thousands of small boats sailed into the Hudson so their owners could watch the parade. Many thousands of people watched from windows and along the river's edge.

What makes a boat float?

When something solid, like a boat, is put into a liquid, like water, the solid pushes some of the liquid aside. If the solid weighs more than the liquid it pushes aside, it will sink. If it weighs less, it will float. A huge, heavy ship floats, too, even though it is made of steel. A big ship contains lots of air, so it weighs less than the water it pushes aside. That is why it floats.

Why are most boats long and narrow?

Long, narrow boats can go through the water quickly. A force called "drag" holds back anything that moves through water. The wider the boat, the more "drag" there is to hold it back. So a long, thin boat can go faster. A boat shaped to get the least possible drag from the water is said to be "streamlined."

230

Do all boats need anchors?

Yes, unless they are tied to a dock. An anchor is a heavy metal object attached to a boat by a long rope. When the anchor is thrown overboard, its pointed hook digs into the bottom of the ocean or the lake. It keeps the boat from drifting away. Before leaving a boat, a good sailor pulls on the anchor, to make sure it has a firm hold in the ground.

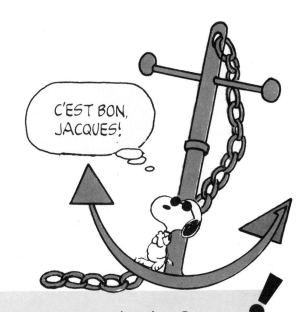

C'EST BON, JACQUES!

The famous ocean scientist Jacques Cousteau (ZHOCK koo-STOE) sank an anchor 24,600 feet (about 7,400 meters) into the Atlantic Ocean!

Jacques Cousteau's research ship, the "Calypso"

What do "knots" mean to a sailor?

Instead of giving speed in "miles per hour" or "kilometers per hour," sailors refer to "knots." A knot equals 1.15 miles per hour. To change from miles per hour to knots, divide by 1.15. For example, 38 miles per hour is the same as 33 knots.

231

ships captains keep logs to burn in the furnace if the weather gets cold.

I FEEL I'M ABOUT TO BE DRAWN INTO A HEATED DISCUSSION!

Why do ships' captains keep logs?

Sally is thinking of the wrong kind of log. A ship's log is the daily record of a trip. The ship's captain is usually the one who keeps the log. The captain writes down all the important details of the trip. These include the exact route, events that happen on board, and radio messages. Over the years, ships' logs have been a great help in piecing together facts about the history of sea travel. A log is also important if a ship has an accident. It helps uncover the reason for the mishap or disaster.

Do ships' captains have road maps to follow?

Yes, in a way. A ship's captain has the help of one or more specially trained people called navigators. Before beginning a voyage, the navigators mark the ship's route on a special sea map, called a chart. During the trip, they keep track of the ship's position by using radar and other electronic equipment. The captain uses this information to stay on the course marked on the chart.

In ancient times, sailors figured out their direction by looking at the stars. Of course, they were in trouble if the sky was cloudy. By the 1100s, sailors were using compasses to tell direction. Today, navigation is much easier. Modern ships rarely get lost at sea.

Section of nautical chart of the Hudson River

How does a compass work?

A compass needle is a magnet. So are the earth's North and South poles. If a compass needle is free to turn, it lines itself up with the earth's magnetic poles. One end points toward the north. The other end points toward the south.

Letters painted on a dial under the needle show all the directions. A sailor just has to look at the compass to see which way the ship is going. For example, if the north end of the compass needle points toward the back of the ship, that means north is behind it. The ship is traveling south.

How does radar help ships?

The word "radar" stands for **ra**dio **d**etecting **a**nd **r**anging. It is a way of telling direction and distance by using radio waves. A radar antenna sends out, in all directions, special signals called radio waves. When these waves bump into a solid object, they bounce back to the antenna. The radar device measures the time it takes for the waves to travel back and forth. Then it figures out where the object is.

Radar will warn a ship's captain—even in a fog—of something in the way of the ship.

What is a buoy?

A buoy (BOO-ee) is a specially shaped or marked float that helps a sailor get around in strange waters. Most buoys are used as channel markers. They warn sailors of shallow or rocky areas or give them other important information. There are also some types of buoys used for mooring (tying up) a boat.

Do any boats move along on the surface of the water?

Two kinds of boats move along on the water's surface—hydrofoils and hovercraft. A hydrofoil skims very quickly over the water. Its hull, or bottom, is just above the surface. Only the hydrofoil's "sea wings" stay in the water. These work very much like airplane wings. When a plane picks up speed, the wings lift it into the air. In the same way, when the hydrofoil picks up speed, its sea wings lift it out of the water. When the boat is in this position, there is less drag from the water. So the hydrofoil can travel much faster than other kinds of boats. Hydrofoils are used for passenger travel and by the military.

Hovercraft—also called air-cushioned vehicles (ACVs)—can be driven on water or land. They have fans or propellers that take in air at the top and blow it out the bottom. A hovercraft is lifted above the surface of the water by the air that comes out under it. These amazing vehicles shouldn't really be called "boats," since they travel above the surface of the water, not in it. Hovercraft can go almost anywhere—swamps, mud, river rapids, ice.

Hydrofoil

What is an iceboat?

An iceboat is a narrow, pointed sail-boat that travels on ice instead of on water. It can do this because it rests on runners—usually three. They look something like short skis. An iceboat's sails are usually very large. They catch the wind and make the iceboat move ahead—just as they would on any sailboat.

Iceboating (also called iceyachting) has long been a favorite pastime in Norway, Sweden, Denmark, and Finland. There the water is frozen most of the year. Today it is a popular winter sport in many other countries as well, including the United States and Canada.

 An iceboat can move twice as fast as the wind!

Can any kind of ship travel through frozen waters?

An icebreaker is a special kind of ship designed to break through ice. Its front section, or bow, is covered with strong metal which acts as armor. Its engines are very powerful. It also has propellers both in back and in front. They make the ship easier to handle than an ordinary ship. To break the ice, the ship's bow climbs partly up on the ice. Its weight causes the ice to break.

The Soviet Union has an atomic-powered icebreaker that can go through 7-foot-thick (2-meter-thick) ice, at 5 miles (8 kilometers) an hour!

U.S. Coast Guard Icebreakers

Has any ship ever sailed to the North Pole?

No ship has ever reached the North Pole on the surface of the water. Ice stops most ships. But one kind of ship can avoid the ice: the submarine, because it moves underwater. In 1958 the nuclear submarine "Nautilus" reached the North Pole by traveling underneath the ice. The next year another nuclear submarine, the "Skate," broke through the North Pole ice.

How does a submarine go up and down?

In order to dive, or go down, a submarine takes water into special storage tanks. The water adds weight to the sub. When the sub gets heavy enough, it sinks. To surface, or go up, air is forced into the tanks to blow out the water. The submarine rises to the surface of the sea. It will stay on the surface until the tanks are flooded with water again.

Once under water, a sub can move upward or downward by using steel fins at the rear of the ship. These are called diving planes. When the fins are tilted down, the submarine will dive. When they are tilted up, the sub will move upward.

I HATE IT WHEN WOODSTOCK PLAYS SUBMARINE IN MY WATER DISH!

How else are submarines used?

Oceanographers (o-she-uh-NOG-ruh-furz)—scientists who study ocean life—use submarines to explore the bottom of the sea. They also use submarines to enable them to get valuable minerals from the ocean floor. Small submarines, called submersibles, are used to explore sunken ships.

What were the first submarines like?

Early submarine experiments date back hundreds of years. In the 1620s, a Dutch engineer built a leather-covered rowing boat that could travel underwater. Twelve men with oars sat inside and rowed. The inventor, Cornelius Drebbel, used some sort of chemical to keep the air breathable. But he kept the formula a secret. So no one knows what it was.

The first submarine ever used in a war was called the "Turtle." It was built and used in 1776 during the American Revolution. It attacked a British warship. But the attack was not successful. The ship did not sink.

The "Turtle" was well named. It was shaped something like a turtle's shell. A man sat inside, turning a pole called a crankshaft. The crankshaft was attached to propellers. When the crankshaft moved, the propellers moved. When the propellers moved, the sub moved.

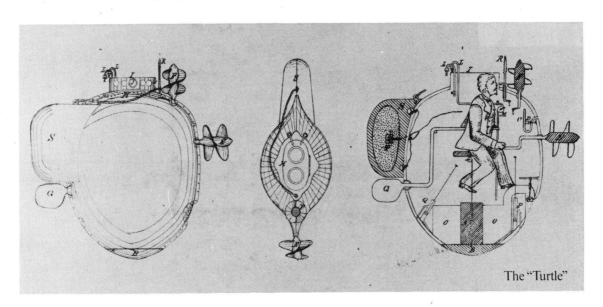

The "Turtle"

How did later submarines solve the air problem?

In the early 1900s, submarines could stay underwater for only short periods of time. The subs did not have any way to replace air. The problem was solved with a snorkel. This is a tube that came out the top of the sub. It allowed fresh air to come into the cabin and to cool the engines. With snorkels, subs could travel for long periods just below the surface of the water. But they could not stay in deep water for more than a few hours at a time.

From sea water, modern submarines can make their own oxygen—the gas we take from the air when we breathe. So the length of time subs can stay underwater does not depend on air supply.

What kind of power do submarines use today?

Modern submarines use nuclear energy. It is the most powerful force known. Uranium (you-RAY-nee-um) is the fuel used for nuclear energy. One ounce (28 grams) of it gives out as much energy as the burning of 100 tons (90 metric tons) of coal. So nuclear-powered subs can travel long distances without refueling.

Are any ships besides submarines powered by nuclear energy?

Yes. Nuclear energy has been used in a few U.S. and Russian ships. But nuclear power for ships is still in the experimental stage. The equipment needed is very bulky. And it's also very expensive. That's why most ships today are powered by diesel or steam engines.

 The "U.S.S. Enterprise," a nuclear-powered ship, can travel more than 200,000 miles (320,000 kilometers) without refueling. That's about eight times around the world!

What's the deepest anyone ever has gone in the ocean?

Nearly 36,000 feet (10,800 meters). Since the 16th century, scientists have used diving bells—round, airtight containers—to go under water. Until recently, these bells were lowered into the water on heavy ropes or steel cables. In 1960, two men went down 35,817 feet (10,745 meters) into the Pacific Ocean. They reached the deepest known part of the ocean. The long trip down took more than five hours. The divers were in a bathyscaphe (BATH-ih-skafe). This is a modern diving bell used to explore the ocean. The bathyscaphe carries heavy steel to make it sink. When the steel is dropped, the bathyscaphe gets lighter so it comes up again. Bathyscaphes carry oxygen in bottles and also chemicals for cleaning used air.

A Bathyscaphe being lowered into the water.

The lights and signals from lighthouses help sailors steer their ships in the right direction. Lightships are floating lighthouses that are permanently anchored near the shore. Their powerful lights and foghorns warn sailors of nearby hazards like rocks or shallow water.

Ships called dredges have special digging tools. They bring up mud and gravel from the bottom of oceans, rivers, or lakes. Dredges are used to make shipping channels deeper and wider so that large vessels can get through. Other dredges are used to dig for valuable minerals or to build up land along the shoreline.

Ship designers test the planned design for a large ship by making a small scale model and testing it in an indoor tank. If there is a problem with the model, it can be solved before construction begins.

The sport of surfing began in the Pacific Islands hundreds of years ago. The first surfboards were made of wood and weighed about 100 pounds. Now surfboards are made of plastic or fiberglass boards and weigh about 30 pounds. Surfers paddle out on their boards to where the ocean waves begin to break. It is possible for a surfer to ride more than a mile on one wave.

Surfers in Hawaii

Inflatable rafts and kayaks are made of heavy cloth that has rubber on one side. They can be stored in small spaces, but they have to be pumped full of air before they will float. Inflatable kayaks bob up and down like ducks in water. That's why they are called "rubber duckies."

Sailors use maps showing high and low places of the ocean floor to help them chart a course. Sailors can't see the floor of the ocean, so they use sound to help them get a picture of it. A depth sounder instrument sends a high-pitched sound that travels to the ocean bottom, from where its echo then bounces back to the surface. The instrument measures how long it takes for the echo to bounce back. If it takes a long time it means that the echo had to bounce back a long distance and that the water is deep. Some depth sounders not only tell the depth of the water—they also use echoes to detect fish!